THE TEACHING
OF JESUS

By REV. LAWRENCE G. LOVASIK, S.V.D.
Divine Word Missionary

CPSIA   June 2013   10 9 8 7 6 5 4 3 2   A/P

NIHIL OBSTAT; Daniel V. Flynn, J.C.D., *Censor Librorum*
IMPRIMATUR: ✚ Joseph T. O'Keefe, D.D., *Vicar General*, *Archdiocese of New York*
© 1981 by Catholic Book Publishing Corp., N.Y.   ISBN 978-0-89942-302-9   Printed in Hong Kong

FAITH AND BAPTISM

The Words of Jesus . . .

NICODEMUS, a ruler of the Jews and a Pharisee, went to Jesus one night and said: "Teacher, we know that God sent You."

Jesus said to him: "Unless a man is born again from above, he cannot see the Kingdom of God."

"How can a man be born again?" asked Nicodemus.

Jesus answered: "No one can enter into God's Kingdom without being born through water and the Spirit.

"God so loved the world that He gave His only Son, that whoever believes in Him may not perish but may have life everlasting.

"God did not send His Son into the world to condemn the world, but that the world might be saved through Him."

The Teaching of Jesus . . .

THE Sacrament of Baptism
gives us new birth as a child of God
made holy by the Holy Spirit.
It makes us share in His Death and Resurrection.
It cleanses us from original sin and personal sins.
It makes us members of His holy Church.

THE BEATITUDES

The Words of Jesus . . .

WHEN Jesus saw the crowds he went up on the mountainside and began to teach them:

"Happy the poor in spirit: theirs is the Kingdom of Heaven. Happy those who mourn: they shall be consoled. Happy the humble: they shall inherit the land.

"Happy those who hunger and thirst for holiness: they shall be satisfied. Happy the merciful: they shall find mercy.

"Happy the sincere of heart: they shall behold God. Happy the peace-makers: they shall be called God's children.

"Happy those who suffer persecution for religion: theirs is the Kingdom of Heaven. Be glad! Yes, be overjoyed: your reward in heaven is great."

The Teaching of Jesus . . .

WE can obtain happiness on earth only by doing good.
We can obtain eternal happiness in heaven
only by following Jesus
and being like Him:
poor, lowly, compassionate, merciful,
holy, pure, peaceable, and patient.

GOOD EXAMPLE

The Words of Jesus . . .

"YOU are the salt of the earth. Suppose salt loses its taste. How can you restore its flavor? It is good for nothing and has to be thrown out.

"You are the light of the world. A city on a mountain top cannot be hidden. People do not light a lamp and then put it under a basket. They set it on a stand where it gives light to all in the house.

"In the same way, your light must shine before men so that they may see your good deeds and give honor to your heavenly Father."

The Teaching of Jesus . . .

A GOOD example means
that we must live according to
the teaching of Jesus
so that people may see
that we are good as Jesus was.
Then we will honor the Heavenly Father.

LOVE OF ENEMIES

The <u>Words</u> of Jesus . . .

"WHEN a person strikes you on the right cheek, turn and offer him the other.

"Give to the man who begs from you. Do not turn your back on the borrower.

"My command to you is this: love your enemies, pray for your persecutors. This will prove that you are children of your heavenly Father, for His sun rises on the bad and the good, and He rains on the just and the unjust.

"If you love those who love you, what merit is there in that. And if you greet your brothers only, what is so praiseworthy about that? Do not pagans do as much?

"You must be made perfect as your heavenly Father is perfect."

The Teaching of Jesus . . .

JESUS teaches us to love everybody,
even those who do not love us,
for the love of God.
Jesus prayed for His enemies on the cross:
"Father, forgive them;
they do not know what they are doing."

PRAYER

The Words of Jesus . . .

"WHEN you pray, go into your own room, close your door, and pray to your Father privately. Then your Father, Who sees what no man sees, will repay you. Your Father knows what you need before you ask Him.

"This is how you are to pray: 'Our Father in heaven, hallowed be Your Name, Your Kingdom come, Your will be done on earth as it is in heaven. Give us today our daily bread, and forgive us the wrong we have done as we forgive those who wrong us. Subject us not to the trial but deliver us from the evil one.'

"Ask, and you will receive. Seek, and you will find. Knock, and the door will be opened to you. For the one who asks always receives. The one who seeks always finds. The one who knocks will always have the door opened to him.

"If you, with all your sins, know how to give your children what is good, how much more will your Heavenly Father give good things to those who ask Him."

The Teaching of Jesus ...

WE should pray
because Jesus taught us to pray,
and because He Himself prayed very often.
The Father wants us to pray
and is always ready to answer our prayers.

TRUST IN GOD

The <u>Words</u> of Jesus . . .

"DO not worry about your life and what you are to eat, nor about your body and how you are to clothe it.

"Look at the birds in the sky. They do not sow or reap or gather into barns; yet your heavenly Father feeds them. Are you not worth more than they are?

"And why worry about clothing? Think of the flowers growing in the fields; they never have to work or spin. Even Solomon in all his glory was not robed like one of these. Now if that is how God clothes the grass in the field which is there today and thrown into the furnace tomorrow, will He not much more look after you, you men of little faith?

"Stop worrying then. Your Heavenly Father knows all that you need. Set your hearts on His Kingdom first, and on His righteousness, and all these other things will be given you as well."

The Teaching of Jesus . . .

GOD is our kind Father. We must trust Him. He will give us all we need in this world, and eternal life in the next.

DOING GOD'S WILL

The Words of Jesus . . .

"IT is not those who say to Me, 'Lord, Lord,' who will enter the Kingdom of Heaven, but the person who does the will of My Father in heaven.

"Therefore, everyone who listens to these words of Mine and acts on them will be like a wise man who built his house on rock. Rain came down, floods rose, and the winds blew and beat against that house, but it did not fall, because it was founded on rock.

"And everyone who hears these My words and does not act upon them will be like a foolish man who built his house on sand. And the rain fell, and the floods came, and the winds blew and beat against that house, and it fell, and was completely destroyed."

When Jesus finished these words the crowds began to believe that He was truly the Christ, the promised Savior.

The Teaching of Jesus . . .

IF we are to answer God's love
we must observe everything
that Christ has commanded,
and believe all that He has taught.
Then we will live as God's children.

HOLY COMMUNION

The Words of Jesus . . .

"I Myself am the living Bread come down from heaven. If anyone eats this Bread he will live forever. And the Bread I shall give is My Flesh, for the life of the world.

"He who feeds on My Flesh and drinks My Blood has life eternal. And I shall raise him up on the last day. For My Flesh is real food and My Blood real drink.

"The man who feeds on My Flesh and drinks My Blood remains in Me, and I in him.

"Just as the Father, Who has life, sent Me and I have life because of the Father, so the man who feeds on Me will have life because of Me.

"This is the Bread that came down from heaven. The man who feeds on this Bread shall live forever."

The Teaching of Jesus . . .

JESUS gives Himself to us
as food for our soul
in Holy Communion.
He also gives us His grace
that we may have His own divine Life
and that we may be able to live
a truly Christian life.
He is the Bread of Life.

JESUS, THE GOOD SHEPHERD

The Words of Jesus . . .

"I AM the Good Shepherd. I know My sheep and My sheep know Me, just as the Father knows Me and I know the Father. And I lay down My life for My sheep.

"I have other sheep that do not belong to this fold. I must lead them, too, and they shall hear My voice, There shall be one flock and one shepherd.

"The Father loves Me because I lay down My life in order to take it up again. No one takes it from Me; I lay it down of My own free will. I have power to lay it down, and I have power to take it up again. This is the command I have received from My Father."

The Teaching of Jesus . . .

JESUS is our Savior and Redeemer
because as God made Man
He gave Himself up to death
out of love for His Father
and for us.

JESUS IS GOD

The <u>Words</u> of Jesus . . .

"I AM the light of the world. Everyone who follows Me will have the light of life and will never walk in darkness.

"When you lift up the Son of Man, you will come to know that I AM. Then you will know that I do nothing by Myself. I say what the Father has taught Me to say.

"The One Who sent Me is with Me. He has not deserted Me, because I always do what pleases Him.

"I came forth from God, and am here. I did not come of My own; it was He Who sent Me. My Father and I are one. I shall remain with you for only a short time now; then I shall go back to the One Who sent Me."

The <u>Teaching</u> of Jesus . . .

JESUS is true God and true Man
because He is God's only-begotten Son,
and in Him there is all fullness of Divinity.
We adore Him
as we adore the Father and the Holy Spirit.

22

THE GREAT COMMANDMENT

The Words of Jesus . . .

A LAWYER asked Jesus: "Which commandment of the law is the greatest?"

Jesus said to Him: "You shall love the Lord your God with your whole heart, with your whole soul, and with all your mind. This is the greatest and the first commandment.

"The second is like it: You shall love your neighbor as yourself.

"On these two commandments the whole Law is based, and the Prophets as well."

The Teaching of Jesus . . .

OUR greatest duty is to do God's will
by keeping His commandments
and living in His love,
and by loving our neighbor as Jesus taught us.
Other words and the example of Jesus tell us
how these commandments are to be practiced.
We are in this world
to know and love and serve God,
and in this way reach
eternal life with God in heaven.

THE HOLY EUCHARIST

The Words of Jesus . . .

JESUS took His place at table, and the Apostles with Him. He said to them: "I have greatly desired to eat this Passover with you before I suffer."

Then, taking bread and giving thanks, he broke it and gave it to them, saying: "This is My Body to be given for you. Do this as a remembrance of Me."

He did the same with the cup after eating, saying: "This cup is the New Covenant in My Blood, which will be shed for you."

The Teaching of Jesus . . .

AT the Last Supper.
Jesus instituted the Eucharistic sacrifice
of His Body and Blood
to continue for all time
the Sacrifice of the Cross
until He would come again.
He gave His Church
a remembrance of His Death and Resurrection.

25

The Teaching of Jesus . . . *(Continued)*

Through the hands of priests
and in the name of the whole Church,
the sacrifice of Jesus is offered
in the Eucharist in an unbloody manner.
The priest, by the sacred power
he receives from Christ,
and acting in His Person,
brings about the Eucharistic sacrifice,
and offers it to God
in the name of all the people.
We receive the Body and Blood of Jesus
in Holy Communion as the food of our soul.

THE NEW COMMANDMENT

The Words of Jesus . . .

JESUS spoke to His Apostles at the Last Supper in these words:

"This is My commandment: love one another as I have loved you.

"There is no greater love than this: to lay down ones's life for one's friends. You are My friends if you do what I command you. I call you friends,

since I have made known to you all that I heard from My Father.

"This is how all will know you for My disciples: your love for one another."

The Teaching of Jesus . . .

JESUS teaches us to love our neighbor
for the love of God and after His example.
One can tell the true Christian
by the love he shows for his fellow man.

THE HOLY SPIRIT

The Words of Jesus . . .

A T the Last Supper Jesus said to His Apostles: "I will ask the Father and He will give
you another Advocate to be with you forever: the

Spirit of truth, Whom the world cannot accept. But you can recognize Him because He remains with you and will be within you.

"The Advocate, the Holy Spirit Whom the Father will send in My Name, will teach you everything and remind you of all that I told you.

"It is for your own good that I go. If I do not go, the Advocate will never come to you. But if I go, I will send Him to you. When He comes He will prove the world wrong about sin, about justice, and about judgment.

"When He comes, being the Spirit of truth, He will guide you to all truth."

The Teaching of Jesus . . .

JESUS promised the Holy Spirit.
He is the Third Person
of the Holy Trinity, really God,
the same as the Father
and the Son are really God.
He is the love of the Father and the Son.

The Holy Spirit came at Pentecost,
never to leave the Church.
He gives His Divine life
of grace to the Church.

GRACE

The Words of Jesus . . .

AFTER the Passover supper, Jesus said to His Apostles: "Make your home in Me, as I make Mine in you. As a branch cannot bear fruit all by itself, but must remain part of the vine, neither can you bear fruit unless you remain in Me.

"I am the vine and you are the branches. He who remains in Me and I in him, will bear much fruit, for apart from Me you can do nothing.

"If you remain in Me, and My words remain a part of you, ask whatever you want and you shall obtain it.

"My Father has been glorified by the fact that you have borne much fruit and become My disciples.

"As the Father has loved Me, so I have loved you. Remain in My love. You will remain in My love if you keep My commandments, even as I have kept My Father's commandments, and remain in His love."

The Teaching of Jesus . . .

THE Sacraments are the ordinary channels of God's grace
and are necessary to keep the life
of grace in our souls.
Jesus gives us His grace
to make us holy,
especially in the Holy Eucharist.

JESUS, OUR TEACHER AND LIFE

The Words of Jesus . . .

"I AM the Way, and the Truth, and the Life; no one comes to the Father except through Me.

"If a man wishes to come after Me, he must deny his very self, take up his cross, and begin to follow in My footsteps."

The Teaching of Jesus . . .

JESUS is our Teacher
and our Way to God.
We must be willing to make sacrifices
for His sake that we may save our soul.